When Mammoths Roamed the Earth

by Alyssa Lauren

SCHOOL PUBLISHERS

Cover, ©Photo Researchers; p.3, ©Pal Hermansen/Stone/Getty Images; p.4, ©David R. Frazier/Photo Researchers, Inc.; p.5, ©CHRISTIAN DARKIN/SCIENCE PHOTO LIBRARY/Photo Researchers; p.6–7, ©Archivo Iconografico, S.A./CORBIS; p.8, p.9, p.10, ©AP Photo/Francis Latreille/Nova Productions; p.11, ©Novosti/Photo Researchers, Inc.; p.12, (tl) ©PhotoDisc, (tr) ©Corbis, (b) ©Jonathan Blair/CORBIS; p.13, (l) ©AP Photo/La Crosse Tribune, Dick Riniker, (r) ©Dave King/ Dorling Kindersley/GETTY IMAGES; p.14, ©Gianni Dagli Orti/CORBIS.

Printed in China

ISBN 10: 0-15-350987-2
ISBN 13: 978-0-15-350987-2

Ordering Options
ISBN 10: 0-15-350601-6 (Grade 4 On-Level Collection)
ISBN 13: 978-0-15-350601-7 (Grade 4 On-Level Collection)
ISBN 10: 0-15-357940-4 (package of 5)
ISBN 13: 978-0-15-357940-0 (package of 5)

4 5 6 7 8 9 10 0940 12 11 10 09

About 40,000 years ago, in a cold land now known as Siberia, large, woolly creatures roamed the Earth. Siberia is in the eastern part of the country of Russia. These creatures, now known as mammoths, were the distant cousins of today's elephants. Mammoths began to die out about 10,000 years ago.

In 1799, a hunter saw some huge bones sticking out of the cold, frozen land of Siberia. Some thought the bones belonged to eerie, huge beasts that lived below the ground. Not many people would go near the bones.

The hunter did not know that the bones belonged to the body of a mammoth. A scientist heard about the bones. The scientist knew the bones were those of a mammoth. Submerged in the ground, the animal's body had been frozen for thousands of years. It still had hairs on its body.

Scientists dug up the bones. They had found the very first whole skeleton of a mammoth. The scientists brought the bones to St. Petersburg, a city in Russia. There they put the bones together to form the skeleton of the mammoth.

People had found mammoth bones before but did not know what they were. Some people thought the bones belonged to an elephant because both elephants and mammoths have tusks and long trunks. Today we know that mammoths were around for thousands of years. They lived all over, too. Mammoth bones have been found in North America, Europe, and parts of Asia.

Mammoths lived during a time called the Ice Age. This was a time when giant sheets of ice covered many northern lands. The Ice Age began about 1.5 million years ago and ended about 10,000 years ago.

Cave paintings of mammoths

At the end of the Ice Age, mammoths and people lived at the same time. People painted pictures of mammoths on cave walls. Early people even hunted mammoths for food. People used the bones to build shelters. Some scientists think that people caught mammoths by trapping them in large pits.

As the Ice Age ended, the land became warmer. The mammoths began to die out. The reasons why mammoths died out are unclear. Some scientists think that mammoths could not live in the warmer climate. Others believe that people hunted too many mammoths, killing them off.

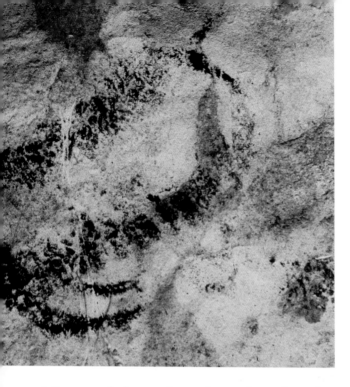

Mammoth bones have been found in the United States. In 1974, in Hot Springs, South Dakota, a worker clearing the land to build houses came across some strange bones. It turned out that they were in a pit that held the bones of nearly one hundred mammoths!

Scientists know a lot about mammoths because many of these animals have been found frozen. The frozen animals have hair and skin. Some of them even have all of their insides, such as the lungs and the heart. Scientists even know what the mammoths ate because they have found food inside their frozen stomachs!

In Siberia, in 1997, a mammoth was found fully buried in ice. Other mammoths had been found in ice before then. To study the animals, scientists melted the ice with hot water from hoses. Often, the hot water ruined the skin and flesh of the mammoths. Only the bones would remain.

This time, scientists wanted to study the whole mammoth, but the process was complicated. Workers used axes and picks to carve out a block of ice in which the mammoth was frozen. Then they put together a contraption to lift the block of ice out of the ground. Ropes were tied to the block of ice. Then the ropes were tied to a helicopter.

Siberia, a part of Russia

The mammoth was flown to a small town in Russia. It was stored in an ice cave. The cave was cold enough to keep the mammoth frozen. There the scientists would begin to study the mammoth.

First, the scientists blew hot air on very small parts of the mammoth using hair dryers. Little by little, the ice around the animal began to melt. They began to see the thick woolly hair of the mammoth. Then, they looked for plants and insects that might have been caught in the mammoth's long hair.

The mammoth was named the Jarkov Mammoth, after the name of the family who found it. Today scientists are still melting the ice around the mammoth. Maybe they will find the insides of the animal. Maybe they will find out how it died. Little by little, as the ice melts, scientists learn more about the Jarkov mammoth.

In 1977, a baby mammoth was found in the frozen ground of Siberia. He was named Dima. Dima still had his skin and some body hair. All of his insides were still there, too! Dima was less than one year old when scientists think he was trapped in the mud. Today Dima's remains are in a laboratory in St. Petersburg in Russia.

Since most mammoth remains are just bones, scientists have to picture what their soft body parts looked like. The frozen mammoths give scientists a good idea of the color of their hair and their skin.

African elephant

Woolly mammoth

Scientists now know that there was more than one kind of these massive animals. The most common mammoth found in the United States is called the Columbian mammoth. It was about the size of a large African elephant.

Another kind was the woolly mammoth. This animal was about the size of an Indian elephant. The woolly mammoth got its name from the long hair that covered its body. Woolly mammoth hair could be up to 3 feet (.91 m) in length! The long woolly hair kept the mammoths warm in the cold environment in which they lived.

Fossil of a
mammoth tooth

All mammoths had long, elegant tusks. One of the longest mammoth tusks ever found came from Texas. It was 16 feet (4.88 m) long. Mammoths used their tusks to fight other mammoths or to dig up food.

Mammoths were plant-eating animals. One mammoth could eat 700 pounds (317 k) of plants in one day! It had only four teeth, but each tooth was about the size of a shoe box! When the teeth wore out, new ones grew. A mammoth grew twenty-four teeth over its lifetime. When the teeth stopped growing, the mammoth was no longer able to eat and would die.

Today scientists face many obstacles when studying animals that lived long ago. One of the hardest things to figure out is how mammoths lived. Scientists believe that mammoths lived in groups called herds. Female mammoths that cared for the young led these herds. When male mammoths were about ten or fifteen years old, they left the herd. Most full-grown males lived alone or in small groups.

One day, scientists may learn why mammoths died out. Knowing what happened to mammoths may help today's animals, too. What people learn from the woolly mammoths that once roamed the Earth may help us save today's animals from becoming extinct!

Think Critically

1. What can scientists learn by studying the remains of mammoths frozen in ice?

2. Why do you think scientists believe that mammoths are the distant cousins of today's elephants?

3. How did scientists transport the Jarkov mammoth to the ice cave in Russia?

4. What is the main idea of this book?

5. Why do you think mammoths became extinct?

 Science

Look It Up Find out more information about woolly mammoths. Then write a paragraph that tells about them. You might also decorate your paragraph with a picture of a woolly mammoth.

 School-Home Connection Tell a family member about the animals you read about in this book. Then talk about what it might be like to find a frozen woolly mammoth.